A Creepy Crawly Story

Vivian French

Illustrated by
Selina Young

Orion
Children's Books

To Lovely Lisa xxx

The stories from *A Creepy Crawly Story* originally appeared in
The Story House first published in Great Britain in 2004
by Orion Children's Books
This edition first published in 2012
by Orion Children's Books
a division of the Orion Publishing Group Ltd
Orion House
5 Upper St Martin's Lane
London WC2H 9EA
An Hachette UK Company

Text copyright © Vivian French 2004 and 2012
Illustrations copyright © Selina Young 2004
Designed by Louise Millar

The right of Vivian French and Selina Young
to be identified as the author and illustrator
respectively of this work has been asserted.

A catalogue record for this book is available
from the British Library

Printed and bound in China

ISBN 978 1 4440 0515 8

www.orionbooks.co.uk

Contents

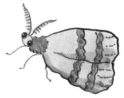

A Creepy Crawly Story

Queen Bee was worried. Where were Wizz Bee and Buzz Bee? The sun was low, and all the other bees were in the beehive.

"Bzzzzzz!" It was Wizz, and his collecting bag was only half full.

"Bzzzzzz!" It was Buzz, and his collecting bag was only a quarter full.

Queen Bee frowned. "This isn't good enough.

How can we make honey if you don't find enough nectar? No dinner for you tonight!"

Buzz flew in a circle. "I collected something else," he said. "I collected a story. A story about a bad butterfly."

Queen Bee looked at him in surprise. "A bad butterfly? Butterflies aren't bad!"

"This one was," Buzz told her.

"Well..." Queen Bee stopped frowning. She loved honey, but she also loved stories.

"It's a very good story," said Wizz. "And there's a bee in it."

Queen Bee nodded. "Very well, then. Tell me the story."

Bad Betty Butterfly

It was Susie Slug's birthday, and she was very excited.

"Can I have a party?" she asked Mummy Slug.

"I don't know, dear," said
Mummy Slug. "What's a party?"

"People come to your house
and bring presents," said Susie.
"They sing 'Happy Birthday to
You' and then you eat cake."
"Oh," said Mummy Slug.
"Well, I suppose we could try."

Susie found a large lettuce leaf. She wrote: "Susie Slug is having a Birthday Party at teatime. Please bring presents. There will be cake."

She left the leaf where everyone could see it, then hurried home to help Mummy Slug.

News of Susie's party spread
round the garden.

"Susie Slug having a party!"
Betty Butterfly fluttered her wings
in surprise. "How horrid!"

Clive Caterpillar looked at the lettuce leaf. "Did you ask her to your birthday party, Betty?" he asked.

"No," said Betty. "Slugs are slimy."

"There's nothing wrong with slime," Stuart Snail said crossly.

"Snails are different," said Betty. "And I'm not going to Susie's party."

"Nor me," said little Mary Moth. She always did what Betty did.

"I like cake," said Stuart, "but I haven't got a present."

"Nor have I," said Clive. "Oh dear."

It was nearly teatime when Bertie Bee came buzzing down to look at the lettuce leaf. "A party!" he said. "Let's all go!"

"We can't," said Clive and Stuart. "We haven't got any presents."

"We don't want to," said Betty and Mary.

"Oh," said Bertie, and he buzzed away to see what Susie was doing.

Susie was looking very sad.
In front of her was a beautiful
cabbage cake.

"Hello," said Bertie.

"Is this where the party is?"

Susie nodded. "Yes," she said, "but it's teatime now, and nobody's come. I'm going to sing Happy Birthday to me, and then I'm going to bed."

"Don't do that!" said Bertie. "I'm sure everybody will come soon."

"Do you really think so?" asked Susie.

"Yes," said Bertie. "Er ... what presents are you expecting?"

Susie wiped away a tear. "I don't know. Betty Butterfly told everyone she had lovely presents at her party.

But then she whispered to Mary that Stuart and Clive gave her some horrid carrot toffee. She said she hid it under a flower pot!"

"Did she?" said Bertie Bee. "How interesting!"

"**Please** don't tell Betty I heard her!" said Susie. "She didn't see me."

"Just give me a minute," said Bertie, "and they'll all be here." He winked at Susie and buzzed off.

Betty Butterfly was showing Mary, Stuart and Clive how lovely her wings looked in the sunshine.

"You're so pretty," said Mary.

"Yes," said Bertie, as he landed beside her. "And I heard you had a birthday last week."

Betty nodded. "Oh yes," she said. "Everybody brought me wonderful presents."

Mary, Stuart and Clive smiled proudly.

"I have so many friends," Betty
said. Then she sniffed. "Not like
that slug."

"Funny you should talk about
Susie," said Bertie. "Are you ready
to come to her party?"

Bertie stared very hard at Betty.
"I'm sure she'd like any kind
of present. She would never be
mean and hide presents under a
flower pot."

Betty stopped flapping her wings, and looked at Bertie. Bertie winked.

"But we don't know anyone like that, do we?" he said.

Betty blushed. Then she smiled her sweetest smile. "But of course we're all going to Susie's party! We'll take her a bunch of daisies!"

"Good idea," said Bertie.
"Now, let's go!"

Betty and Mary and Bertie flew to Susie Slug's party, while Clive and Stuart hurried between the cabbages.

And Susie Slug had the best party ever.

Queen Bee smiled. "Bees always know what to do," she said. "That was a good story. Where did you hear it?"

Buzz fluttered his wings. "Wizz and I were by the pond. Mrs Frog was telling stories to her tadpoles."

"By the pond?" Queen Bee sounded very cross indeed. "You should have been in the flower garden!"

"It was the wind," Buzz said quickly. "It blew us towards the pond. And Mrs Frog told another story too. It was about a very brave moth. "

"Moths aren't brave." Queen Bee was still cross.

"This one was," Wizz told her. "Very brave!"

Queen Bee looked at Buzz, and then at Wizz. She knew it hadn't been a windy day, but she did love stories.

She nodded. "Very well, then. Tell me the story."

Brave
Mary Moth

One spring evening, Clive
Caterpillar was chatting with his
friends.

"When I'm a butterfly," he said,
"I'll fly higher than any butterfly
has ever flown before."

"Oooooh!" Susie Slug went pale. She was frightened of heights.

"Oh, Clive!" said Mary Moth. "You'll get very dizzy!"

"Not me," boasted Clive. "I'll fly up and up until I can see the top of the clouds."

"Height isn't everything," said Stuart Snail. "Last week I slithered from one end of the garden to the other."

"It took you four days," said Clive. "When I'm a butterfly I'll fly from one end of the garden to the other in two minutes."

"Oh, Clive!" said Mary Moth. "You'll get very tired!"

"No I won't," said Clive. "In fact, I'll probably fly all the way round the world and back by dinnertime."

Betty Butterfly came fluttering by and stopped to listen.

"What are you going to do by dinnertime, Clive?" she asked.

Clive blushed bright pink. "Nothing," he said.

"He says he's going to fly all the way round the world and back," said Stuart.

"Could you fly all the way round the world, Betty?" Susie Slug asked.

"I expect I could if I wanted to," said Betty, and she stretched her wings.

"Ooooh!" Susie said. "You're wonderful, Betty."

"Of course she couldn't," said Stuart. "Really! Sometimes I think you'd believe anything, Susie."

Betty frowned at Stuart. "It's too late to fly round the world tonight," she said. "I could fly to the big tree down by the stream and back."

"But it's getting dark," Mary Moth said anxiously.

Betty fluttered her wings. "I'll be back before the stars come out," she said. And off she flew.

Susie, Stuart, Mary and Clive sat and waited.

And waited.

And waited.

The light faded away, and stars began to twinkle in the dark blue night sky.

"She's not back yet," said Susie in a very small voice. "Do you think she's all right?"

Stuart was feeling guilty, and it made him cross. "Don't fuss, Susie."

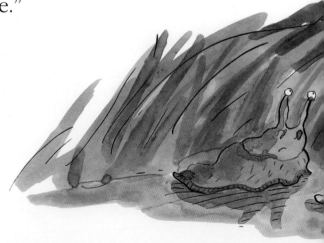

"Maybe I should go and look," said Mary Moth.

"YOU?" Clive said. "What could you do?"

"Well … moths can see in the dark," Mary said. And she fluttered away.

"Oh dear," said Susie, and a tear slid down her nose. "Betty is gone for ever! Oh dear, oh dear!"

"I think you and Clive should go home," said Stuart. "Just leave it to me."

"I'm too worried about Betty and Mary to go home on my own," Susie said.

"I'm going to sleep," Clive said, and he wriggled under the leaves.

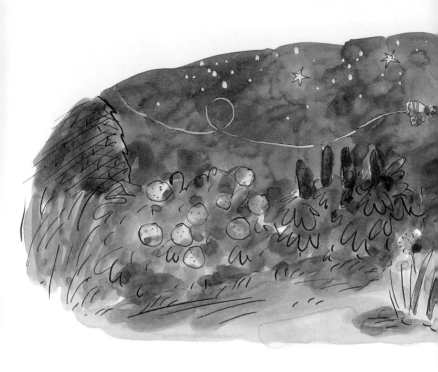

Mary Moth flew down the garden towards the big tree. As she flew she listened, but she could hear nothing until…

"Help!"

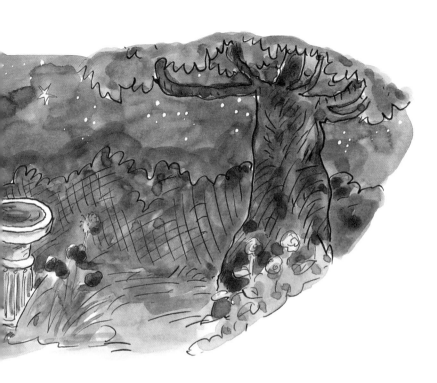

Mary headed towards the rose bushes. She was almost sure the voice had come from there. Then she heard it again.

"Help!"

That's Betty! thought Mary. "Where are you, Betty? I'm coming!"

There was a loud sniff from the roses.

"I've flown into a spider's web," Betty said. "Be careful, Mary!"

Mary could see Betty now. She was stuck in the middle of a large web, which was hanging on a rose bush. She looked very unhappy.

"Hmm," said Mary. "I think we need Stuart. He's good at climbing."

"Stuart?" Betty flapped her wings. "Oh, don't tell Stuart. He'll just say how silly I am."

"I'm sure he won't," Mary said in her kindest voice.

"He will!" Betty wailed. "And he'll be right!"

Mary didn't answer. She was thinking. If Stuart climbed up the rose bush and jumped into the web, he would break it.

"I'm sorry, Betty," Mary said, "but we really do need Stuart."

"I'm here!" said a voice.

Mary was so surprised she flew straight into the spider's web.

"Oh no!" gasped Betty. Now Mary was caught too.

Below, Stuart coughed. "Sorry. Didn't mean to frighten you. What can I do to help?"

Mary stayed very still.
"Stuart," she said. "You must climb up the rose bush as high as you can. Then jump. That will break the web, and Betty and I will be free."

"Jump?" Stuart could hardly believe his ears. "Me? A snail? Jump?"

"Well, fall then," said Mary. "Please, Stuart."

Stuart slid slowly across the grass. He was not a happy snail.

"I only wanted to surprise them," he muttered. "I didn't mean to make Mary fly into the web. And now they want me to jump. I wish I'd never got out of bed this morning."

He began to climb slowly up the rose bush.

"Up," he panted. Up! Up and up!"

Higher and higher Stuart climbed. The web trembled.

"Oh!" said Betty. "Is the spider coming?"

"No," said Mary. "It's Stuart. He's nearly at the top. He'll be jumping any minute now. We'll soon be free, Betty."

Stuart clung to the highest branch. He knew he had to jump. It was just that the branch kept moving to and fro.

"Ooooooh!" said Stuart. "I feel sick!" He shut his eyes.

"It's all right, Stuart," said a tiny voice. "I'll jump with you."

Stuart opened his eyes wide.
It was Susie Slug. She was right beside him. She looked as cool as a cucumber.

"Ready?" asked Susie. "One – two – three – GO!"

Halfway down, Stuart wondered
if Susie had pushed him. But
he didn't have time to decide,
because at that moment the two
of them burst through the web.

The web broke and Betty
and Mary fluttered free!

All the way home Betty and Mary told Stuart and Susie how wonderful they were. Susie glowed with pride.

"Stuart the Super Snail," said Betty.

"Susie the Super Slug," said Mary.

 "I only followed Stuart because I didn't want to be left on my own," Susie said.

Stuart suddenly stopped. "I've just worked something out," he said.

 "What's that, Stuart?" asked Betty.

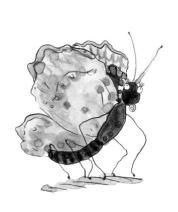

"If Mary hadn't come to find you, you wouldn't be here now," said Stuart. "So we should thank Mary too."

"Brave Mary Moth to the rescue!" said Susie.

"It was nothing," said Mary, and she blushed.

There was a rustling of leaves near by. A sleepy voice said, "When I'm a butterfly I'll fly up to the moon and back. Nobody will ever need to rescue me!"

Queen Bee smiled.
"That's a good story."

"Yes," said Buzz. "But if I was there, I would have saved the butterfly myself."

"You can't see in the dark," said Queen Bee. "And it's getting dark now, so it's bedtime."

Wizz looked hopeful. "Can we have something to eat first?"

Queen Bee shook her head. "You didn't collect enough nectar."

"But we collected two stories," said Wizz. "And they made you smile. You don't smile when we bring you nectar."

There was a silence. Then Queen Bee laughed. "Well done, Wizz," she said. "Yes. You and Buzz can both have some dinner, but you must work extra hard tomorrow!"

"We will," said Wizz.

"We promise," said Buzz.

And they flew away quickly before Queen Bee could change her mind.